This book
belongs to:

Mom Works Too!

Text: *Jennifer Moore-Mallinos*

Illustrations: *Marta Fàbrega*

BARRON'S

My name's Emma and I'm six years old. Yesterday, at school, our teacher talked to us about moms who work outside the home. My teacher said that even though most dads went to work everyday, so did a lot of moms.

And what a surprise it was to hear the teacher say that she also was a mother!

I guess my teacher was right, because when she asked the class to put their hands up if their moms left the house every morning to go to work, almost everybody raised their hand. And since both my Mom and Dad work, I put my hand up too!

At home, Mom told
me that she used to
work as a secretary
in an office before I was born.
Now that I am older she went
back to her old job. And even
though being a mom is what she
likes best, she loves her work also.

Mom and Dad said that when I was born they were very happy. They always wanted to be parents. Mom got maternity leave (that means getting excused from your job) and she stayed home for three months so she could take good care of me. I don't remember this because I was too little, but Mom likes to tell stories about how much fun we had together.

During class yesterday, when we
were talking about working moms,
one of the kids asked why did
both parents have to work. Our
teacher said that parents love
their children and want to

give them a nice home,
pretty clothes, and
other good things, but
all that is expensive and
so both the mother and the father
often have to go to work.

Some kids only have a mother or a father. My friend, Jacob, lives with his mom, and she goes to work every day. She wants to make sure that Jacob has all the things he needs, like food, a place to live, and even  money for the bus. Jacob and I love taking swimming lessons together, especially since we're in the same class!

Today, when I came home from school, my babysitter, Hannah, was waiting for me in the kitchen. As usual there was a snack sitting on the table for me. Hannah told me that Mom and Dad would be home early today because they had a surprise for me. I couldn't wait to find out what the surprise was so I asked Hannah twice, but she just smiled and said nothing at all.

While I sat on the steps of the porch waiting
for Mom and Dad, I started to think about

what my surprise was going to be.
Maybe it was going to be that bike
that I keep asking for or maybe they
changed their minds and decided to
let me have a dog. I always wanted
a dog. I even picked out his name—Lucky.

It seemed like it took forever, but Mom and Dad finally came home. As soon as I saw them, I ran over and gave them both a hug and started asking about my surprise. I couldn't wait to find out what it was! Then Dad took my hand and put it on Mom's tummy and said "Guess what? You're going to be a big sister soon!"

At first I didn't know what to say. I was so surprised!
It was so exciting to think that soon I would have a
 brother or a sister that I almost forgot about
wanting a puppy, until Mom asked me what
I thought the surprise was going to be.

Mom said that she knew I wanted to have a puppy very much and that maybe when my baby brother or sister gets a bit bigger we'd get a puppy then.

I thought that was a great idea, because I'm going to
be busy helping Mom and Dad with the baby, and maybe
it would be too much work to have both a baby and
a puppy at the same time.

Mom said that after the baby is born she was going to take a maternity leave and stay home for a while to look after the baby, just like she did with me when I was little. And then when the baby gets a bit older, she was going to go back to work and Hannah would look after us.

Wow! I can't wait to be a big sister! There are so many things I want to show my sister or brother, like how to build a tower out of blocks or how to stay in the lines when you're coloring, and when he or she gets older, I'll be able to explain why both Mom and Dad go to work every day. Hey, maybe my sister or brother will love taking swimming lessons just as much as I do!

Note to parents

All mothers are working moms! Whether a woman stays at home to raise her family or works outside the home, all mothers work and their jobs are important.

Although some women have the opportunity to decide between staying home and working outside the home, there are many women who don't have a choice. Financial restraints often force both parents to seek employment. There are also one-parent families where the parent has to work outside the home in order to support his or her family.

Having both parents working outside the home is a way of life for many children. Just like adults, children want to know why things are the way they are. Therefore, it is important to take the time to explain to children the reasons that surround our decision to work. Whether a mother's decision to work outside the home is motivated by financial demands or is based purely on her enjoyment of the job, neither can be viewed as wrong and it is good that children recognize that.

A parent's decision to work can be influenced by many things, such as lifestyle, financial circumstances, and personal goals. Since every family is unique, decisions made within families will vary significantly, but no decision should be judged as being either right or wrong but rather be measured regarding its usefulness for all concerned.

As we learned in the text, a mother's life is not always bound to include just one role. Many mothers take on other roles, such as that of a teacher or a secretary. Being a mother doesn't mean that you must stop being all the other things you already are or aspire to be, and it's good for children to recognize that. Some children may find it difficult to believe that their mother can or would want to find enjoyment in other aspects of her life, such as working outside the home. Most children see their mother as a mother and nothing else. Some are even surprised to learn that their mother is not only a mother but a woman as well!

Although one's motivation or reason for working outside the home may differ, there are several commonalities that exist among working parents. For example, many parents who are returning to the workforce after being home for a period of time may experience feelings of guilt when leaving their child. However, once a routine is established and a level of comfort is acquired between the child, the parents, and the alternate caregiver, everybody will feel better.

It's true that working parents are confronted with many obstacles they're expected to manage. Finding a balance between work schedules, demands at the workplace, and responsibilities at home is a continuous struggle for many working parents. Not to mention finding and maintaining appropriate childcare arrangements, making time for family activities, and, last but not least, finding time for themselves and each other.

Another common worry among working parents is choosing the right caregiver for their child. Choosing a caregiver that will provide quality care can be a difficult process and it's one that all working parents can relate to. Whether it's a daycare setting, a live-in babysitter, or a babysitter within the community, making sure that the care environment is suitable for their child is of the greatest importance for all parents. It may seem like a long drawn-out process when it comes to choosing the best daycare provider for your child, but just knowing that your child is in capable hands during the day will make everybody more at ease. So take the time to investigate your options; it's worth it!

We hope that after reading this text your children will have a better understanding of the many reasons that explain a family's decision for both parents to work outside the home. It only seems fair that we provide children with as much information as they can handle in order for them to feel more comfortable with their daily routine.

MOM WORKS TOO!

First edition for the United States and Canada published
in 2008 by Barron's Educational Series, Inc.
© Copyright 2008 by Gemser Publications S.L.
El Castell, 38; Teià (08329) Barcelona, Spain (World Rights)
Title of the original in Spanish: *¡Mi mamá también trabaja!*
Phone: 93 540 13 53
E-mail: info@mercedesros.com
Author: Jennifer Moore-Mallinos
Illustrator: Marta Fàbrega

All inquiries should be addressed to:
Barron's Educational Series, Inc.
250 Wireless Boulevard
Hauppauge, New York 11788
http://www.barronseduc.com

ISBN-13: 978-0-7641-4042-6
ISBN-10: 0-7641-4042-6
Library of Congress Control Number 2007941410

Printed in China
9 8 7 6 5 4 3 2 1